A GIFT FOR CHRISTMAS

Michael O'Mara Books Limited

First published in Great Britain in 2001 by
Michael O'Mara Books Limited
9 Lion Yard
Tremadoc Road
London SW4 7NQ

Researched by Jacquie Wines, Vanessa Williams and Isabel Nohan

The publisher would like to thank David Drummond for his help in researching illustrative material.

Picture permissions
Cover picture and pages: 4, 15, 28, 31, 32, 40, 42 used by permission of Mary Evans Picture Library
Pages: 6, 9, 11, 12, 16, 17, 18, 19, 25, 27, 30, 38, 39, 45, 47 used by permission of David Drummond

Page 14: Extract from *Cider With Rosie* by Laurie Lee published by Hogarth Press.
Used by permission of The Random House Group Limited.
Page 17: Poem used by permission of The Literary Trustees of Walter de la Mare and
the Society of Authors as their representative.
Page 25: Extract from Penguin UK edition of *Love For Lydia* by H. E. Bates used
by permission of Laurence Pollinger Limited and the Estate of H. E. Bates

A CIP catalogue record for this book is available from the British Library

ISBN 1-85479-984-3

1 3 5 7 9 10 8 6 4 2

Designed by Mick Keates

Printed and bound in Singapore by Tien Wah Press

CONTENTS

It was on
Christmas Day

It was on Christmas Day,
And all in the morning,
Our Saviour was born,
And our heavenly king:
And was not this a joyful thing?
And sweet Jesus they called him by name.

ANON

THE LEGEND OF THE BEASTS
IN THE STABLE

It is said that in the stable where Mary bore Jesus, alongside the donkey that had carried her to Bethlehem, there were also some oxen sheltering from the winter cold. That evening the animals were all given some hay, but they didn't eat it, knowing that it would be needed to make a bed for the soon-to-be-born baby.

Once the child arrived, the beasts gathered around and breathed on him gently to keep him warm, and when the shepherds came to worship the babe, the animals too knelt down before the manger. Later, the donkey noticed some mice and rats in the stable and he was concerned for the baby, and started to bray to keep them away. But this woke the baby, so the oxen began to low softly to lull him back to sleep.

It is said that to repay the animals for their loving kindness, they were granted the power of human speech every year at the midnight that comes between Christmas Eve and Christmas Day. Some believe that this is still so, and that every Christmas Eve, at midnight, the animals in the fields kneel down to worship the Christ child.

BETHLEHEM OF JUDEA

A little child,
A shining star.
A stable rude,
The door ajar.

Yet in that place,
So crude, forlorn,
The Hope of all
The world was born.

ANON

I Saw Three Ships
Come Sailing In

I saw three ships come sailing in
On Christmas Day, on Christmas Day.
I saw three ships come sailing in
On Christmas Day in the morning.

And what was in those ships all three
On Christmas Day, on Christmas Day?
And what was in those ships all three
On Christmas Day in the morning?

Our Saviour Christ and His lady
On Christmas Day, on Christmas Day.
Our Saviour Christ and His lady,
On Christmas Day in the morning.

Pray whither sailed those ships all three
On Christmas Day, on Christmas Day?
Pray whither sailed those ships all three
On Christmas Day in the morning?

O, they sailed in to Bethlehem
On Christmas Day, on Christmas Day.
O they sailed in to Bethlehem
On Christmas Day in the morning.

And all the bells on earth shall ring
On Christmas Day, on Christmas Day.
And all the bells on earth shall ring
On Christmas Day in the morning.

And all the angels in Heav'n shall sing
On Christmas Day, on Christmas Day.
And all the angels in Heav'n shall sing
On Christmas Day in the morning.

And all the souls on earth shall sing
On Christmas Day, on Christmas Day;
And all the souls on earth shall sing
On Christmas Day in the morning.

Then let us all rejoice again
On Christmas Day, on Christmas Day.
Then let us all rejoice again
On Christmas Day in the morning.

WORDS: ENGLISH TRADITIONAL

GOOD KING WENCESLAUS

There actually was a King Wenceslaus. He was born in about AD 903 into the Premys family, who were the most able of the Bohemian nobles, and who ruled over various tribes. Bohemia, which was then a duchy rather than a kingdom, had forged links with the German Holy Roman Emperor and the Duke supported and encouraged the spread of Christianity.

However, Wenceslaus's mother, Dragomir, was a pagan, and she was violently against her husband's beliefs. She eventually overthrew him and had many Christian missionaries killed. But she was, in turn, overthown, and the Christian Wenceslaus, as the eldest son, was installed as Duke. Dragomir did not accept this course of events and encouraged her younger son, Boleslav, to wage war on Wenceslaus. This he did, but legend has it that Wenceslaus was protected by an angelic bodyguard during battle.

Wenceslaus won and he recalled the German missionaries and promoted Christian beliefs throughout Bohemia. He became famous for his generosity, charitable deeds and selfless behaviour.

As tradition has it, on the feast of Stephen – which falls on 26th December and commemorates St Stephen, the first Christian martyr – Wenceslaus stood at his castle window looking out at the snowy landscape. Darkness had fallen, but the moon was bright and in its light Wenceslaus could discern the figure of an old man, bent and in rags, who was struggling to pick up firewood.

Wenceslaus was moved with pity for the man and called to his old servant to come to him. He asked the servant if he knew the poor man and where he lived. The servant informed him that he lived against the forest fence near the fountain of St Agnes. Wenceslaus then asked the servant to fetch meat and wine, while he himself shouldered some large logs of wood, and the two of them set off to the poor man's home. The wind was so chill and the snow was so deep that after a time the old servant called out that he could go no farther. But Wenceslaus turned and smiled encouragement on him and told him to walk close behind him so that he would be sheltered from the winter wind and could walk in his footsteps. To the old servant's amazement, he found that when he did as Wenceslaus bade him, the deep snow ceased to hamper him, and despite the shrill whistling of the wind he could continue onwards.

In reward for Wenceslaus's efforts, Emperor Otto I upgraded Bohemia to a kingdom and

presented Wenceslaus with a crown, which can still be seen today. On 28 September 929, as King Wenceslaus was praying, he was ambushed by Boleslav, who murdered him at the church door. Wenceslaus was hailed as a martyr and was canonized and installed as the patron saint of Bohemia. Boleslav was crowned king and ruled until 967. However, he was overcome with remorse at having killed his brother, and converted to Christianity. Therefore, Bohemia remained Christian.

THE STORY OF SILENT NIGHT

In Salzburg, Austria, a weaver called Anna fell in love with a soldier and she conceived a child who was born on 11 December 1792. The soldier wanted nothing to do with his son and he abandoned Anna, leaving her to bring up the boy on her own. She named him Joseph Mohr.

Not only was Joseph an intelligent child, he had a lovely voice. The local priest arranged for him to

attend the famous abbey school of Kremsmünster, and later, when he was sixteen, he decided to go into the priesthood. At the age of twenty-two he was assigned to the church of St Nicholas in Oberndorf, just outside Salzburg.

There Joseph became friends with a local music teacher, Franz Gruber, for they both shared a love of music and both played the guitar.

On 23 December 1818, Joseph went to visit a mother and her newborn child. On his way back, he stopped by the river and reflected on the very first Christmas. He wrote a poem to capture his thoughts and called it 'Silent Night'.

On arriving back at the church, he found the parish in a state of alarm. Some mice had nibbled away at the church organ and the villagers were fearful that there would be no music for Midnight Mass the following evening.

Joseph had an idea. He rushed to his friend Franz Gruber and asked if he could compose a melody for the poem he had written, to be played on the guitar. Franz worked on the song and completed it in time for the mass. So it was that Christmas, that the world first heard the well-loved carol that is now sung in many languages across the globe.

SILENT NIGHT

JOSEPH MOHR

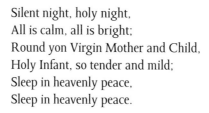

Silent night, holy night,
All is calm, all is bright;
Round yon Virgin Mother and Child,
Holy Infant, so tender and mild;
Sleep in heavenly peace,
Sleep in heavenly peace.

Silent night, holy night,
Shepherds quake at the sight;
Glories stream from heaven afar,
Heavenly hosts sing alleluia;
Christ the Saviour is born,
Christ the Saviour is born.

CAROL SINGING

LAURIE LEE, from *Cider with Rosie*

We grouped ourselves round the farmhouse porch. The sky cleared, and broad streams of stars ran down over the valley and away to Wales. On Slad's white slopes, seen through the black sticks of its woods, some red lamps still burned in the windows.

Everything was quiet; everywhere there was the faint crackling silence of the winter night. We started singing, and we were all moved by the words and the sudden trueness of our voices. Pure, very clear, and breathless we sang:

> *As Joseph was a walking*   *He neither shall be bornèd*
> *He heard an angel sing;*   *In housen nor in hall,*
> *'This night shall be the birth-time*   *Nor in a place of paradise*
> *Of Christ the Heavenly King.*   *But in an ox's stall . . . .'*

And two thousand Christmases became real to us then; the houses, the halls, the places of paradise had all been visited; the stars were bright to guide the Kings through the snow; and across the farmyard we could hear the beasts in their stalls. We were given roast apples and hot mince-pies, in our nostrils were spices like myrrh, and in our wooden box, as we headed back for the village, there were golden gifts for all.

DECK THE HALLS WITH BOUGHS OF HOLLY

We often use foliage to decorate our homes at Christmas. Green foliage symbolizes the continuance of life through the dark winter months, and in a Christian context the eternal life offered to us by Christ. The tradition of placing a wreath of greenery on the door of the house probably dates back to Roman times, when wreaths were hung as a sign of spring's victory over winter.

Holly also has a symbolic meaning. The prickly leaves of the holly bush represent the crown of thorns worn by Jesus at his crucifixion and the red berries symbolize the drops of blood that he shed. Mistletoe was considered by Celtic druids to be a sacred plant and sprigs of it were used as charms. Its dark green leaves and white berries are often found hanging from the ceiling at Christmas, but be careful – anyone who wants to kiss you may do so if you are standing under the mistletoe.

MISTLETOE

WALTER DE LA MARE

Sitting under the mistletoe
(Pale green, fairy mistletoe),
One last candle burning low,
All the sleepy dancers gone,
Just one candle burning on,
Shadows lurking everywhere:
Some one came, and kissed me there.

Tired I was; my head would go
Nodding under the mistletoe
(Pale green, fairy mistletoe),
No footsteps came, no voice, but only,
Just as I sat there, sleepy, lonely,
Stooped in the still and shadowy air
Lips unseen – and kissed me there.

17

THE SHEPHERD
WHO STAYED BEHIND

On the night when Jesus was born, there were shepherds in the fields around Bethlehem tending their flocks. Suddenly a mighty throng of angels appeared to them and bade them go visit the Christ child.

The shepherds hurried away, but one shepherd, Shemuel, stayed behind. He longed to join the others as they rushed down the hillside and into the town, but earlier in the evening he had found a sick man lost in the hills. Shemuel had cared for him all night. The man was certainly close to death and it would not be fair to leave him.

When the other shepherds came back from the town telling of the babe in the stable who would be Lord of All, Shemuel was filled with great sadness that he had not been there.

Soon afterwards he became ill with the stranger's fever, and realized that he too was going to die. He was terrified and bitter at his fate. However, as Shemuel lay on the ground a most wondrous sight appeared above him. There in the sky was a vision of God the Father, God the Son and God the Holy Ghost, seated on high.

As he gazed, all of Shemuel's fear and disquiet left him. Although he had been unable to see the Christ child, he was the first among men to be shown the Holy Trinity. Shemuel closed his eyes and his spirit left him and was guided up to Heaven by the angels.

SOFTLY THE NIGHT

Softly the night is sleeping on Bethlehem's peaceful hill,
Silent the shepherds watching their gentle flocks are still.
But hark the wondrous music falls from the opening sky,
Valley and cliff re-echo glory to God on high.
Glory to God it rings again,
Peace on the earth, goodwill to men.

Come with the gladsome shepherds quick hastening from the fold,
Come with the wise men bringing incense and myrrh and gold,
Come to him poor and lowly all round the cradle throng,
Come with our hearts of sunshine and sing the angels' song.
Glory to God tell out again,
Peace on the earth, goodwill to men.

Wave you the wreath unfading, the fir tree and the pine,
Green from the snows of winter to deck the holy shrine;
Bring you the happy children for this is Christmas morn,
Jesus the sinless infant, Jesus the Lord is born.
Glory to God, to God again,
Peace on the earth, goodwill to men.

ANON

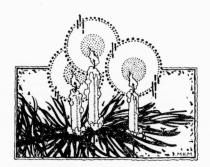

XMAS DAY

G. K. CHESTERTON

Good news: but if you ask me what it is, I know not;
It is a track of feet in the snow,
It is a lantern showing a path,
It is a door set open.

WINTER FESTIVITIES

The middle of winter has long been a time of celebration around the world. Centuries before the birth of Christ, Europeans celebrated light and birth in the darkest days of winter. Many people rejoiced during the winter solstice when the worst of the winter was behind them and they could look forward to longer days and extended hours of sunlight.

The end of December was a perfect time for celebration in most areas of Europe. At that time of year, most cattle were slaughtered so that they did not have to be fed during winter. For many, it was the only time of the year when they had a supply of fresh meat. In addition, most wine and beer was finally fermented and ready for drinking.

In Rome, where winters were not as harsh as those in the far north, Saturnalia, a holiday in honour of Saturn, the god of agriculture, was celebrated. Beginning in the week leading up to the winter solstice and continuing for a full month, Saturnalia was a hedonistic time, when food and drink were plentiful.

Around the time of the winter solstice, Romans also observed Juvenalia, a feast honouring the children of Rome. In addition, members of the upper classes often celebrated the birthday of Mithra, the god of the unconquerable sun, on December 25. It was believed that Mithra, an infant god, was born of a rock. For some Romans, Mithra's birthday was the most sacred day of the year.

WINTER IN-DOORS AND OUT

Out of doors warm hoods and mittens
Cheeks with romping all a-glow
Merry slides and splendid skating
Harmless tumbles in the snow
In the house a cosy nook
And a tempting story book.

Out of doors a snow-man funny
On a sled a journey gay
In the house a smoking dinner
Dolls to dress and games to play
Races in the frosty air
In the house an easy-chair.

Out of doors the cold wind blowing
Snow-drifts piling in the street
In the house the rosy firelight
Rest for weary hands and feet
Darkness out of doors and din
Home and mother safe within.

ANON

WINTER

WILLIAM SHAKESPEARE

When icicles hang by the wall
    And Dick the shepherd blows his nail,
And Tom bears logs into the hall,
    And milk comes frozen home in pail;
When blood is nipt, and ways be foul,
Then nightly sings the staring owl
          Tu-whit!
Tu-who! A merry note!
While greasy Joan doth keel the pot.

When all about the wind doth blow,
    And coughing drowns the parson's saw,
And birds sit brooding in the snow,
    And Marian's nose looks red and raw;
When roasted crabs hiss in the bowl —
Then nightly sings the staring owl
          Tu-whit!
Tu-who! A merry note!
While greasy Joan doth keel the pot.

SKATING AT CHRISTMAS

H. E. BATES, from *Love for Lydia*

'There'll be skating,' she said. 'That would be wonderful – skating for Christmas. Everybody loves the idea of skating for Christmas. Everybody waits for it and it hardly ever comes.'

We came to a small hill where the road made a passage between spinneys of oak and hazel above the valley of a brook. The delicate branches of hazel, fingered already with pale stiff catkins, were snowless under the high protective screen of oaks. Where the sun caught them the catkins were pale greenish-yellow, almost spring-like, and I could see the primrose leaves piercing a crust of snowy oak-leaf under thin blue shadows. The hill was not very steep but Blackie put the car into lower gear, driving with a new excess of caution, so that we crept down into the valley at less than walking pace, the ghostly, glittering chariot making hardly a sound in the closed avenue of hazels.

Then we were clear of the woods and suddenly, delicate and transfigured and untouched, the river valley of snow-meadows, with small lakes of frozen flood water lying darker about it, was there below us. It appeared so suddenly and was so beautiful, full in sun, the snow deep blue below the paler blue of sky and between the tawny-purple lips of frosty horizons, that she sat bolt upright in her seat and let go my hands.

'Oh! stop – let's stop here! That's so lovely —'

A Christmas Husbandly Fare

Thomas Tusser, 1573

Good husband and huswife, now chiefly be glad.
Things handsome to have, as they ought to be had.
They both do provide, against Christmas do come,
To welcome their neighbours, good chere to have some.

Good bread and good drinks, a good fier in the hall,
Brawne, pudding, and souse, and good mutard withal.
Biefe, mutton, and Porke, and good Pies of the best,
Pig, veale, goose and capon, and turkey wel drest,
Chese, apples and nuttes, and good Caroles to heare,
As then, in the country is counted good cheare.
What cost to good husbande, is any of this?
Good household provision onely it is:
Of other the like, I do leave out a meny,
That costeth a husband never a peny.

IT IS NOW CHRISTMAS...

NICHOLAS BRETON, 1626

It is now Christmas, and not a cup of drink must pass without a carol: the beasts, fish and fowl come to a general execution, and the corn is ground to dust for the bakehouse and the pastry – Now good cheer and welcome, and God be with you.

SNAP-DRAGON – A VICTORIAN CHRISTMAS GAME

… a kind of play, in which brandy is set on fire, and raisins thrown into it, which those who are unused to the sport are afraid to take out, but which may be safely snatched by a quick motion and put blazing into the mouth, which being closed, the fire is at once extinguished.

BRITISH POPULAR CUSTOMS (1876)

It should be said that the Victorians were much more cavalier about safety than their 21st century counterparts.

CHRISTMAS EVE

WASHINGTON IRVING, from Old Christmas and Bracebridge Hall

As we approached the house, we heard the sound of music, and now and then a burst of laughter from one end of the building. This, Bracebridge said, must proceed from the servant's hall, where a great deal of revelry was permitted, and even encouraged, by the Squire throughout the twelve days of Christmas, provided everything was done conformably with ancient usage . . .

Supper was announced shortly after our arrival. It was served up in a spacious oaken chamber, the panels of which shone with wax, and around which were several family portraits decorated with holly and ivy. Beside the accustomed lights, two great wax tapers, called Christmas candles, wreathed with greens, were placed on a highly-polished buffet among the family plate. The table was abundantly spread with substantial fare; but the Squire made his supper of frumentt, a dish made of wheat cakes boiled in milk with rice spices, being a standing dish in old times for Christmas Eve. I was happy to find my old friend, the minced-pie, in the retinue of the feast; and finding him to be perfectly orthodox, and that I need not be ashamed of predilection, I greeted him with all the warmth wherewith we usually greet an old and very genteel acquaintance.

Glorious Plum Pudding

In a household where there are five or six children, the eldest is not above ten or eleven, the making of the pudding is indeed an event. It is thought of days, if not weeks, before. To be allowed to share in the noble work, is a prize for young ambition … Lo! The lid is raised, curiosity stands on tip-toe, eyes sparkle with anticipation, little hands are clapped in extasy, almost too great to find expression in words. 'The hour arrives – the moment wished and feared;' – wished, oh! how intensely; feared, not in the event, but lest envious fate should not allow it to be an event, and mar the glorious concoction in its very birth.

And then when it is dished, when all fears of this kind are over, when the roast beef has been removed, when the pudding, in all the glory of its own splendour, shines upon the table, how eager is the anticipation of the near delight! How beautifully it steams! How delicious it smells! How round it is! A kiss is round, the horizon is round, the earth is round, the moon is round, the sun and stars and all the host of heaven are round. So is plum pudding.

THE ILLUSTRATED LONDON NEWS, December 1848

THE STORY OF THE CHRISTMAS CRACKER

We must thank Tom Smith for the Christmas cracker. Tom was a London confectioner who was always looking for novel ideas. He travelled abroad in search of inspiration and brought back the bonbon to England after a trip to France. His bonbons contained a motto beneath their wrapping – probably a Victorian love poem – and the sweets sold very well, particularly at Christmas. In 1847, Tom was sitting by his fire, musing on ways to increase trade, when the sparks from the crackling logs gave him an idea. He would invent a bonbon that went off with a bang when opened, and inside would be not only a sweet but also a motto and a toy. He named these *cosaques*, but today we still talk of bonbons in connection with Christmas crackers.

Tom Smith enjoyed huge success with his crackers and soon had a royal warrant. He produced crackers not only at Christmas but also for every special occasion, including the Paris Exhibition in 1906 and the Prince of Wales's World Tour in 1926.

LOVE CAME DOWN
AT CHRISTMAS

CHRISTINA ROSSETTI

Love came down at Christmas,
    Love all lovely, love divine,
Love was born at Christmas,
    Star and angels gave the sign.

Worship we the Godhead,
    Love incarnate, love divine;
Worship we our Jesus:
    But wherewith for sacred sign?

Love shall be our token,
    Love be yours and love be mine,
Love to God and all men,
    Love for plea and gift and sign.

TRUCE IN THE
TRENCHES, 1914

W. R. M. PERCY, LONDON RIFLE BRIGADE

We had a rather interesting time in the trenches on Christmas Eve and Christmas Day. We were in some places less than a hundred yards from the Germans, and we talked to them. It was agreed in our part of the firing line that there should be no firing and no thought of war on these days, so they sang and played to us several of their own tunes and some of ours, such as 'Home Sweet Home' and 'Tipperary' etc., while we did the same for them.

The regiment on our left all got out of their trenches and every time a flare went up they simply stood there, cheered and waved their hats, and not a shot was fired on them. The singing and playing continued all night, and the next day (Christmas) our fellows paid a visit to the German

trenches and they did likewise. Cigarettes, cigars, addresses etc. were exchanged, and everyone, friend or foe, were real good pals. One of the German officers took a photo of English and German soldiers arm in arm, with exchanged caps and helmets.

On Christmas Eve the Germans burnt coloured lights and candles along the top of their trenches, and on Christmas Day a football match was played between them and us in front of the trench. They even allowed us to bury all our dead lying in front, and some of them, with hats in hand, brought in one of our dead officers from behind their trench so that we could bury him decently. They were really magnificent in the whole thing, and jolly good sorts. I have now a very different opinion of the German. Both sides have now started firing and are deadly enemies again. Strange it all seems, doesn't it?

SOLDIERS' SONG

It was Christmas Day in the cookhouse,
The happiest day of the year,
Men's hearts were full of gladness,
An' their bellies full of beer . . .

THE SNOW LIES WHITE

The snow lies white on roof and tree,
Frost fairies creep about,
The world's as still as it can be,
And Santa Claus is out.

He's making haste his gifts to leave,
While the stars show his way,
There'll soon be no more Christmas Eve,
Tomorrow's Christmas Day!

ANON

ST NICHOLAS'S SCARY HELPER

Most people have heard of St Nicholas as Santa Claus or Father Christmas, but few have heard about his scary helper. In the Netherlands he is called Black Peter, in Germany he is Knecht Ruprecht, in France he is known as Pere Fouettard and in Luxembourg they call him Hoesecker.

While St Nicholas comes to give all the good children presents, his helper puts switches in the stockings of the naughty girls and boys for their parents to spank them with. Some say that he even carries away those who have been really naughty in his bag.

EPIPHANY

The word Epiphany comes from the Greek word *epiphaneia*, which means an appearance or a manifestation. In the Greek and Russian orthodox churches, Christmas is celebrated on January 6, which is also referred to as Epiphany or Three Kings Day. This is the day it is believed that the three wise men found Jesus in the stable in Bethlehem.

THE THREE KINGS

The Three Kings are also known as the Wise Men or the Magi. Traditionally they were Caspar, King of Tarsus, the Land of Myrrh; Melchior, King of Arabia, the Land of Gold; and Balthasar, King of Saba, the Land of Frankincense.

The gifts of Gold, Frankincense and Myrrh are all symbolic. Gold symbolizes kingship, and also the gift of charity and spiritual riches embodied in Christ. Frankincense depicts godliness and the gift of faith. Myrrh foretells the painful death of Jesus and the gift of truth and meekness.

Although the Wise Men returned home after visiting Jesus some say they were baptized by St. Thomas and later became Christian martyrs, and that their bodies were buried within the walls of Jerusalem.

Twelfth Night and the Lord of Misrule

Twelfth Night marks Epiphany in the Church's calendar. Through the ages, Twelfth Night has been a time when the existing social order is turned upside-down. This can be found both in the Roman festival of Saturnalia and the Babylonian festival of Sacaea, where servants became masters and the masters had to obey their slaves.

In the fifth century, the churches of France and England carried on this tradition, appointing Bishops and Archbishops of Fools to revel and cause mischief. This continued in England until the Middle Ages, where a beggar or student would be crowned the 'Lord of Misrule' and the poor would go to the homes of the rich and demand the very best food and drink. Failure to comply with this request would probably result in the household being terrorized with mischief.

In the Netherlands, a version of this tradition continues to this day. On 6 January, which is known as *Driekoningendag* or Three Kings Day, an Epiphany cake is baked and whoever finds the bean inside it is king for the day and wears a gold paper crown.

THE YULE LOG

In Scandinavia, because it is so far north, the sun disappears from the sky in the middle of winter. Before people understood why it was dark in winter, they were frightened that one year the sun might go away and never come back, so after thirty-five days of darkness scouts were sent on to the mountains to look out for the return of the sun. When the sun had been sighted, the scouts would return to their villages with the good news and Yuletide would begin. The sons and fathers of families would go out and find a large log, or Yule log, which they would then set on fire. Yuletide celebrations would continue until the log had finished burning – sometimes this could go on for twelve days! The Norse believed that every spark that the fire made represented the birth of a new pig or calf during the next year. As the fire began to die down, a piece of the Yule Log would be taken out and saved until the next year, when it would be used to light the next Yule Log.

CHRISTMAS IN A VILLAGE

JOHN CLARE

Each house is swept the day before,
And windows stuck with evergreens;
The snow is bosomed from the door,
And comfort crowns the cottage scenes.
Gilt holly with its thorny pricks
And yew and box with berries small,
These deck the unused candlesticks,
And pictures hanging by the wall.

Neighbours resume their annual cheer,
Wishing with smiles and spirits high
Glad Christmas and a happy year
To every morning passer-by.
Milkmaids their Christmas journeys go
Accompanied with favoured swain,
And children pace the crumping snow
To taste their granny's cake again.

Hung with the ivy's veining bough,
The ash trees round the cottage farm
Are often stripped of branches now
The cottar's Christmas hearth to warm.
He swings and twists his hazel band,
And lops them off with sharpened hook,
And oft brings ivy in his hand
To decorate the chimney nook . . .

The shepherd now no more afraid,
Since custom does the chance bestow,
Starts up to kiss the giggling maid
Beneath the branch of mistletoe
That 'neath each cottage beam is seen
With pearl-like berries shining gay,
The shadow still of what has been
Which fashion yearly fades away.

And singers too, a merry throng,
At early morn with simple skill
Yet imitate the angel's song
And chant their Christmas ditty still;
And 'mid the storm that dies and swells
By fits – in hummings softly steals
The music of the village bells
Ringing round their merry peals.

And when it's past, a merry crew
Bedecked in masks and ribbons gay,
The morris dance their sports renew
And act their winter evening play.
The clown-turned-king for penny praise
Storms with the actor's strut and swell,
And Harlequin a laugh to raise
Wears his hunchback and tinkling bell.

And oft for pence and spicy ale
With winter nosegays pinned before,
The wassail singer tells her tale
And drawls her Christmas carols o'er,
While prentice boy with ruddy face
And frost-bepowdered dancing locks
From door to door with happy pace
Runs round to claim his Christmas box.

ROBIN REDBREAST'S SONG

There was once a robin with a beautiful voice who wanted to sing for the King on Christmas morning. It was a long way to the castle, but the robin was determined to get there.

He flew and he flew until he came to rest in a tree. Just then a cat came to sharpen its claws on the trunk. 'Good morning Robin Redbreast,' said the cat. 'Where are you going on this cold day?' 'I'm going to the King,' answered the robin, 'to sing him a Christmas song.' 'Oh, but wait before you go,' said the cat. 'Fly down and I'll show you the beautiful collar my owners gave me today.' The robin was tempted, but he saw the cruel gleam in the cat's eye. 'Thank you, good Cat,' he said, 'but I must fly straight on to the King. Merry Christmas to you.'

He flew on and on and finally rested on a fence. There sat a hawk. 'Good morning, Robin Redbreast,' cried the hawk. 'Where are you going on this cold day?' 'I'm going to the King,' answered the robin, 'to sing him a Christmas song.' 'Oh, but wait before you go,' said the hawk. 'Pray spare a moment to see my magic tail feather.' The robin was tempted, but he noticed the way that the hawk was flexing his talons. 'Thank you, good Hawk,' he said, 'but I must fly straight on to the King. Merry Christmas to you.'

So he spread his wings and flew away. He flew, and he flew, and he flew, till he came to a hillside and rested on a mound. A fox looked out from his hole. 'Good morning, Robin Redbreast,' said the fox. 'Where are you going on this cold day?' 'I'm going to the King,' answered the robin, 'to sing him a Christmas song.' 'Wait a while and catch your breath,' said the fox. 'I will come closer and warm you with my winter coat.' The robin was cold and tired, but he saw how the fox was licking his lips. 'Thank you, good Fox,' he said, 'but I must go straight on to the King. Merry Christmas to you.'

So the robin flew away once more, and never rested till he came to a small boy, who sat on a log eating a big piece of bread and butter. The robin was very hungry by now and he hoped that the boy might throw him a crumb. 'Good morning, Robin Redbreast,' said the boy. 'Where are you going on this cold morning?' 'I'm going to sing a Christmas song to the King,' said the robin. 'Come a bit nearer,' said the boy. 'I'll give you some crumbs from my bread.' The robin was very grateful, but suddenly he spotted the stones in the boy's hand.

'Thank you, good Sir,' he said, 'but I must fly straight on to the King. Merry Christmas to you.'

So, no matter who begged him to stop and wait, the robin flew straight on to the King. And finally he alighted on the window-sill of the palace. There he sat and sang the sweetest Christmas song he knew. He wanted the whole world to be as joyful about Christmas as he, and he sang, and he sang, and he sang.

The King and Queen were so pleased with his joyful song that they asked all the courtiers what they could give the robin in return. It was decided that they should find the robin a mate. Thus they brought to him Jenny Wren, who lived in the kitchen courtyard, and the two birds sang all that Christmas and many Christmases thereafter.

GERMAN CAROL

The Christmas tree with lights is gleaming,
And stands in bright and festive glow.
As if to say – Mark well my meaning.
Hope's image green and bright I show.

A CHRISTMAS WELCOME

CHARLOTTE BRONTË, from *Jane Eyre*

'My first aim will be to clean down ... Moor House from chamber to cellar; my next to rub it up with beeswax, oil, and an indefinite number of cloths, till it glitters again; my third, to arrange every chair, table, bed, carpet, with mathematical precision; afterwards I shall go near to ruin you in coals

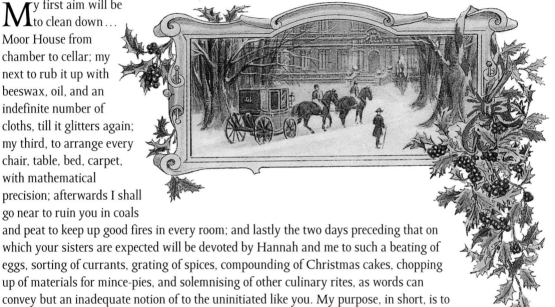

and peat to keep up good fires in every room; and lastly the two days preceding that on which your sisters are expected will be devoted by Hannah and me to such a beating of eggs, sorting of currants, grating of spices, compounding of Christmas cakes, chopping up of materials for mince-pies, and solemnising of other culinary rites, as words can convey but an inadequate notion of to the uninitiated like you. My purpose, in short, is to have all things in an absolutely perfect state of readiness for Diana and Mary before next Thursday; and my ambition is to give them a beau-ideal of a welcome when they come.'

Jane Eyre to St. John Rivers

MOONLESS DARKNESS STANDS BETWEEN

GERARD MANLEY HOPKINS

Moonless darkness stands between.
Past, O Past, no more be seen!
But the Bethlehem star may lead me
To the sight of Him who freed me
From the self that I have been.
Make me pure, Lord: Thou art holy;
Make me meek, Lord: Thou wert lowly;
Now beginning, and alway:
Now begin, on Christmas Day.